My Jewish World
An Early Childhood Music Curriculum

My Jewish World

An Early Childhood Music Curriculum

Judy Caplan Ginsburgh

UAHC Press
and
Transcontinental Music Publications
New York, New York

My Jewish World CD is available separately
from the UAHC Press and Transcontinental Music
at 888-489-UAHC or www.transcontinentalmusic.com

Table of Contents

Acknowledgments

Many thanks to Joel Eglash, Martha Katz, Cantor Josée Wolff, and Rabbi Hara Person for your faith and trust in me with this project. Thanks to Liane Broido for getting a great cover and working on the manuscript. And thanks to everyone at the UAHC Press and Transcontinental Music for helping bring this project into being, including Ken Gesser, Stuart Benick, Rick Abrams, Debra Hirsh Corman, Rachel Gleiberman, Mark Dunn, Karen Schatz, Michael Kaplan, and Eric Komar. Thanks to Beth and Steve Meltzer for their hospitality and for schlepping me all over Boston. Thanks to Peter and Ellen Allard for a fun evening and yummy dinner. Thanks to Rabbi Arnold Task for rabbinic assistance. Thanks to Cheryl Cohen for her assistance and suggestions with art ideas, Isabel Baker of The Book Vine for her book suggestions, and Lois Grant with the Rapides Parish Library for her assistance with sources. Special thanks to Josh Nelson; every minute of working with you was a pleasure and a privilege. And thanks to all of the songwriters who contributed to this project. You, above all, know how much music can mean in a child's life. To all of the teachers and parents who are listening, teach your children to sing and share music with your children each and every day.

Introduction

Young children are constantly learning and discovering things about their world. A Jewish child's world includes being Jewish, and not just on Shabbat and holidays. Judaism should and can be integrated into everything we do. Our Jewish classrooms can provide a foundation for a proud Jewish identity and a model for Jewish living. As teachers, we must help children discover the "Jewishness" in everything they do.

Music is something that is basic and enjoyable to all children. Much can be learned and mastered through musical "play." Just as we should strive to incorporate Judaism into our everyday world, we should also incorporate music as much as possible. Music can serve as a catalyst, it can introduce or wrap up a lesson, it can progress a lesson, it can facilitate easy transitions, it can help to explain, it can help us remember, and it can, simply, make learning more fun!

In order to develop a Jewish early childhood music curriculum, my task was to seek out songs that would help young children learn about daily things that happen in a Jewish preschool classroom. Dozens of songwriters, both Jewish and non-Jewish, were contacted and asked to submit material for the project. Our committee listened to hundreds of songs. Finally, the choices were narrowed down to what you have here—music that can enhance and motivate learning about being Jewish each and every day.

The book contains music to all songs featuring melody line, lyrics, and chords. It also contains creative ideas for teaching each concept to young children. For each topic, an objective is stated, followed by comments and creative ideas.

Also included for many of the topics in this curriculum are suggested books to enhance learning. Encourage children to look at, listen to, and read books. Encourage them to make their own books. You may even want to create a "Jewish Learning Book" incorporating Hebrew words and prayers that you have learned throughout the year. Just through the songs in this curriculum alone, you will learn about Torah, the mezuzah, *tzedakah,* being a mensch, *shalom,* body parts, numbers, colors, and more.

So, go ahead—create your Jewish world!

Wake-Up Sh'ma

Objective

• To introduce children to the *Sh'ma* prayer.

Comments

The *Sh'ma* is the essential prayer of our Jewish faith. It is important for children to know and feel comfortable with this prayer from an early age. We often associate the *Sh'ma* with bedtime, but this lively version of the *Sh'ma* helps us start our day with the knowledge that *Adonai* (God) is always with us. The word *sh'ma* means "hear" or "listen."

שְׁמַע יִשְׂרָאֵל: יהוה אֱלֹהֵינוּ, יהוה אֶחָד!

Sh'ma Yisrael: Adonai Eloheinu, Adonai Echad!
Listen, O Israel: *Adonai* is our God, *Adonai* is One!

Ideas

Sh'ma Prayer Plaque

1. Trace each child's hand on a piece of heavy-stock paper.

2. Glue a piece of paper with the *Sh'ma* prayer written on it in the middle of the hand.
3. Cut out the hand and glue it onto a piece of colorful mat board (you can often buy mat board scraps at hobby or frame shops) so that there is a nice border around the hand.
4. Have children decorate their hand plaques with crayons, glitter, sequins, etc. Have them try not to put decorations on the prayer.
5. Punch a hole in the top and add a piece of yarn, string, or cord for hanging.

God Is Always Here With Us

Sing or play the song, and then ask the children to tell you how they know that *Adonai* is always here. Ask the children to name some ways that we see God's work in our world.

Nature Walk

Take the class on a morning nature walk, and encourage students to point out God's beautiful creations that you see or hear along the way. Write them down. You may even want to create a classroom poster with pictures of what you saw and heard.

Being a Friend

Talk about friends and how to be a friend by sharing, helping, listening, including, and so on.

Suggested Book

Wake Up! by Sandra Boynton. New York: Workman Publishing Company, 2000.

Wake Up Sh'ma

Music & Lyrics: Hanna Tiferet

I wake up__ each morn-ing__ with love in__ my heart for the world and__ the peo-ple I know. I pray for__ the cour-age__ to be who__ I am and to make friends__ wher-ev-er I go. Sh'-ma Yis-ra-eil, A-do-nai E-lo-hei-nu.__ Sh'-ma Yis-ra-eil, A-do-nai E-chad. Sh'-ma__ Yis-ra-eil, A-do-nai E-lo-hei-nu.__ Sh'-ma Yis-ra-eil, A-do-nai E-chad.

God Made All Living Things: Modeh Ani

♪♪♪♪♪♪♪♪♪♪♪♪♪♪♪♪♪

Objectives

- To introduce children to the *Modeh Ani* prayer.
- To get children into a habit of thanking God each morning.

Comments

The *Modeh Ani* prayer is said upon waking in the morning to thank God for the world and all the things around us. The prayer can teach children to have "awe" and respect for life and all living things. The words *modeh ani* mean "I give thanks." You may also want to sing *modah ani,* the feminine form of the phrase.

מוֹדֶה (מוֹדָה :קרשצקכ) אֲנִי לְפָנֶיךָ, מֶלֶךְ חַי וְקַיָם

שֶׁהֶחֱזַרְתָּ בִּי נִשְׁמָתִי בְּחֶמְלָה, רַבָּה אֱמוּנָתֶךָ.

Modeh ani l'fanecha melech chai v'kayam shehechezarta bi nishmati b'chemlah rabbah emunatecha.

I give thanks to You, O God, O everlasting Creator, for You have returned my soul to me in mercy. Great is Your faithfulness.

6

Ideas

Differences

This song can be a catalyst for a discussion of differences. There are many different-looking people and creatures in the world. God made them all and loves them all. We are all connected by God.

Modeh Ani Chain

1. Make a paper chain out of construction paper rings (symbolizes that we are all connected).
2. Have the children draw, cut out pictures, or write about things they are thankful for. Have them write or glue these things on cutouts of various colors and shapes.
3. Punch a hole at the top of each shape (you may want to laminate them first).
4. Put a piece of string or yarn through the hole, and then tie it around a link in the paper chain.
5. Display somewhere in the classroom.

Suggested Book

All Kinds of Children, by Norma Simon, illustrated by Diane Paterson. Morton Grove, Ill.: Albert Whitman, 1999.

God Made All Living Things: Modeh Ani

Music & Lyrics: Rachel Sumner
Hebrew adaptation: Judy Caplan Ginsburgh

God made all liv-ing things. Mo - deh a - ni.
*(Trees and bugs and me.)

God made all liv-ing things. Mo - deh a - ni.
(Beaut - i - ful to see.)

Diff'-rent col - ors, diff'-rent siz - es. God made things that way.

That is why we should be thank - ful ev' - ry sin - gle day.

God made all liv - ing things Mo - deh a - ni.
(Beaut - i - ful, it's true.)

God made all liv - ing things. Mo - deh a - ni.
(Trees and bugs and you.)

* Words in parentheses are from original,
English-only, version of this song.

8

Boker Tov/Good Morning

Objectives

- To get children acquainted with each other and with you.
- To help everyone learn each other's names.
- To introduce the students to some basic Hebrew phrases.

Comments

This song can be used at the beginning of the year to help learn everyone's names. It is a good tool for reinforcing listening skills. It can also be used to make a smooth transition to another activity. Feel free to add additional verses like "Good morning to all of my friends . . . ."

Ideas

Zipper Song

The second part of the song can be used as a "zipper" song. You can insert individual names into the song to welcome everyone in the class. When you first introduce the song, "zip" in only one name each time you sing it (example: "Good morning, good morning to Aaron. Good morning, good morning to Aaron. Good morning, good morning to Aaron. Good morning, good morning to Aaron . . ."). Repeat this using each child's name. Encourage the other students to sing along as a welcome to each child. As children get more familiar with one another's names, "zip" a different name in after each "Good morning" phrase (example: "Good morning, good morning to Rachel. Good morning, good morning to Sara . . .").

Greeting Each Child

1. Have children sit in a circle on a carpet square or on tags with their names that have been taped to the floor.
2. Sit or kneel in the center of the circle, and work your way around the circle singing each child's name.
3. As you sing to each child, make sure you shake their hand or make physical contact with them in some way as a form of welcome. This helps to break down the space barrier and lets them know that you are okay.

Facilitating Transitions

The song can also be used to facilitate transitions. Explain to the children that when they hear you sing their name in the song, they should go to a particular place (e.g., to the table, to a center). This will encourage them to listen and then respond in an orderly fashion (example: "Good morning, good morning to Alyssa, you can go to the table now. Good morning, good morning to Josh, you can go to the table now").

Suggested Book

Good Morning, Boker Tov, by Michelle Abraham, illustrated by Selina Alko. New York: UAHC Press, 2001.

Boker Tov Means Good Morning

Music & Lyrics: Sherrie Stohl
& Judy Caplan Ginsburgh

Bo ker tov, bo - ker tov means good morn - ing. Rise and shine, bo - ker tov, bo - ker tov. Bo-ker tov, bo - ker tov means good morn - ing. Rise and shine, bo - ker tov, bo - ker tov. When you see your friends you say sha - lom cha - vei - rim. Bo - ker tov, sha - lom sha - lom!

Good Morning

Music & Lyrics: Bobby Susser
(Hebrew added by Judy Caplan Ginsburgh)

Good morn-ing, good morn-ing to you. Good morn-ing, good morn-ing to you. Good morn-ing, good morn-ing to you. Bo-ker tov, bo-ker tov to you. Bo-ker tov, bo-ker tov to you. Bo-ker tov, bo-ker tov to you.

Thanks God!

♪♪♪♪♪♪♪♪♪♪♪♪♪♪♪♪♪♪

Objective

• To talk about the wonder of and workings of our bodies.

Comments

Each morning Jews thank God for their bodies and the miraculous way in which they function. Our heart pumps blood through our body. This is what helps to keep us alive. We eat for nourishment and energy. Our body uses what it needs to keep us going, and what we do not need comes out of our bodies as waste. This is a simple song that can lead to as much or as little conversation as you want to have concerning bodily functions, using the potty, and hygiene. The words *n'kavim* and *chalulim* mean "openings" or "vessels." When air, blood, food, or waste travels through the openings and vessels in our bodies, then we work properly.

בָּרוּךְ אַתָּה יְיָ, אֱלֹהֵינוּ מֶלֶךְ הָעוֹלָם, אֲשֶׁר יָצַר אֶת־הָאָדָם

בְּחָכְמָה, וּבָרָא בוֹ נְקָבִים נְקָבִים, חֲלוּלִים חֲלוּלִים.

Baruch atah Adonai, Eloheinu Melech haolam, asher yatzar et haadam b'chochmah uvara vo n'kavim n'kavim, chalulim chalulim.

13

Praised are You, *Adonai* our God, Creator of the universe, who has made our bodies with wisdom, combining veins, arteries, and vital organs into a finely balanced network.

Ideas

Feeling Your Heart Beat

1. Ask children to jump up and down in place ten times. Have them count as they do it.
2. Now ask them to be very quiet and put their hands over their heart. See if they can feel their hearts beating and pumping blood through their bodies.
3. Have them try to feel other pulse points on their bodies.

Feeling Air Going In and Out of Your Body

1. Have children lie on the floor on their backs.
2. Coach them to breathe in (inhale) and be aware of their chests rising and filling up with air.
3. Now have them breathe out (exhale). They should notice their chest and stomach getting flatter. Breathing helps our bodies work, just like when you put air in (inflate) a tire, it helps the car run.

Suggested Books

On Your Potty, by Virginia Miller. Cambridge, Mass.: Candlewick Press, 2000.

Potty Time, by Guido Van Genechten. New York: Simon & Schuster, 2001.

Everyone Poops, by Taro Gomi, translated by Amanda Mayer Stinchecum. La Jolla, Calif.: Kane/Miller Book Publishers, 1993. (Graphic.)

Look Inside Your Body, by Gina Ingoglia and Mario Gomboli, illustrated by Carlo Michelini. New York: Grosset & Dunlap, 1998. (Explains parts of the body, including muscles, blood, bones, and anatomical sexual differences.)

Thanks God!

Music & Lyrics: Andy Curry
(based on Asher Yatzar blessing)

1. Thanks God!__ I seem to be wor-king fine.__ You made me with a grand de - sign.__ N' - ka - vim__ __ n' - ka - vim cha - lu - lim__ cha - lu - lim. Thanks God!__ I seem to be wor-king fine.__

Additional lyrics:

2.   Thanks God! for lungs and sto-mach and heart.
     For all my a-ma-zing parts.
     N'-ka-vim n'-ka-vim cha-lu-lim cha-lu-lim.
     Thanks God! I seem to be wor-king fine.

3.   Thanks God! blood is rush-ing through my veins.
     From my toes up to my brain.
     N'-ka-vim n'-ka-vim cha-lu-lim cha-lu-lim.
     Thanks God! I seem to be wor-king fine.

Shalom Shalom

♪♪♪♪♪♪♪♪♪♪♪♪♪♪♪♪♪

Objective

- To introduce children to the versatility of the word *shalom*.

Comments

Shalom is a great Hebrew word. It proves that Jews never really say good-bye—even when we say good-bye, we are really saying hello. And we are always wishing everyone peace.

Ideas

Expressing Hello and Good-bye Physically

1. Talk about the different ways we express hello and good-bye with our bodies. (Example: Some people wave, some people hug, some people kiss, some people shake hands, some people have sad faces when they say good-bye, etc.)
2. Act out various ways to express hello and good-bye.

Shalom Door Hangers

Premade door hanger shapes are available in wood and plastic at craft stores, or paper ones can be purchased from specialty paper catalogs. Have children color them with paint or markers and then decorate them with rubber stamps (try to find some Jewish ones, especially one that says *shalom*), stickers, glitter, etc.

Fill In the Blanks

When you sing the song, leave out certain words and let the children fill them in.

Going in, going _____ or coming home

Hello, _____, peace to everyone.

Going _____, going out or coming _____

We say _____, *shalom.*

This will help children remember the song and get used to the various meanings of *shalom.*

Expressions

Try to say *shalom* with different feelings and expressions. Have the children try to say it like they are happy to see someone, like they don't want to say good-bye, and like they are shy. Have them say it loud, say it high, say it soft, say it low, etc.

Shalom Shalom

Music & Lyrics: Fran Avni

Sha - lom,_____ sha - lom,_____ sha - lom,_____ sha - lom._____ Sha - lom,_____ sha - lom,_____ sha - lom,_____ sha - lom. lom. Go-ing in, go - ing out, com - ing home.___ Hel - lo, good - bye,___ peace to ev - ery - one.___ Go - ing in, go - ing out, or com - ing___ home,___ we say sha - lom,_____ sha - lom. Go - ing lom.

18

My Body is Part of Me

Objective

- To teach children the names of various parts of their bodies in English and in Hebrew.

Comments

Our bodies are wonderful things. We all occupy a certain space. Our bodies come in a variety of sizes, and we all move in different ways. This song will help develop coordination, memory, and movement skills. It can also provide an opportunity for discovering spatial relations.

Ideas

What Can You Do?

Discuss how we take care of our bodies. What things can you do all by yourself? With what do you need help?

Our Feet Were Made for Walking

1. Ask children to remove their shoes and socks. Roll up pant legs.
2. Lay out a large piece of butcher paper on the floor.

3. Place one disposable aluminum pan or paint tray filled with washable tempra paint on one side of the paper and another pan filled with soapy water on the other side of the paper along with some towels.
4. Have each student step in the paint pan and walk across the paper to the other side. (You may want to have their first step be on some paper towels to blot the paint.)
5. Label at least one of their footprints with their name.
6. When they reach the other side of the paper, have them step in the pan with the soapy water to clean their feet and dry off with a towel.
7. Hang the poster of the walking feet in the hallway.

Body Double

1. Have each child lay on a piece of butcher paper on the floor, and trace around each child's body.
2. Cut the tracings out and mount them on the walls of the classroom or hallway.
3. Type or write the names of various body parts in English or Hebrew on small slips of paper and cut them out. Do one set for each child, and give each child a set. At the same time, make a master set on large index cards for yourself.
4. Hold up your large card with a body part word written on it.
5. Children must find the matching word from their slips of paper.
6. When they find the correct body part name, they may go and glue, tape, or Velcro it onto their traced body in the proper place, or
7. As children learn a body part in Hebrew or English, have them label it on their body picture. When they have mastered all of the body parts, they can bring their complete body picture home.

Body Assembly

Have children assemble a movable cardboard body puzzle using brads to connect the pieces, or

1. Cut out body parts, and attach stick-on magnets to each part.
2. Put all the parts in a box.
3. Ask children to pick parts out of the box and assemble them part by part on a magnetic board until they have put together a whole "person."

My Space

Have children do various movement activities, and have them become aware of the space occupied by their bodies. Some activities need more space. Have them move forward, backward, sideways, up, and down.

What Can You Do with Your Body?

Ask children to think about various parts of their bodies and what they can do.

> With my hands I can: clap, reach, write, grab, touch, etc.
> With my feet I can: walk, kick, run, jump, etc.
> With my mouth I can: eat, talk, kiss, etc.
> With my head I can: think, nod, etc.

Relationships

1. Make game cards with pictures of various body parts on them (e.g., eyes, nose, head, mouth). Make one card for each child.
2. Make individual smaller cards with pictures of objects that relate to these various body parts (e.g., glasses—eyes; box of tissue—nose; hat—head; ice-cream cone—mouth).
3. Give each child a game card and a set of smaller cards, and ask them to place the proper related objects on the game cards.

Suggested Books

I'm Growing, by Aliki. Scranton, Pa.: Harper Collins Childrens Books, 2001.

Here Are My Hands, by Bill Martin, Jr., and John Archambault, illustrated by Ted Rand. New York: Henry Holt, 1989.

My First Body Board Book, by Iris Rosoff, Shaila Awan, and Helen Melville. New York: DK Publishing, 2000.

My Body is Part of Me

Music & Lyrics: Peter & Ellen Allard

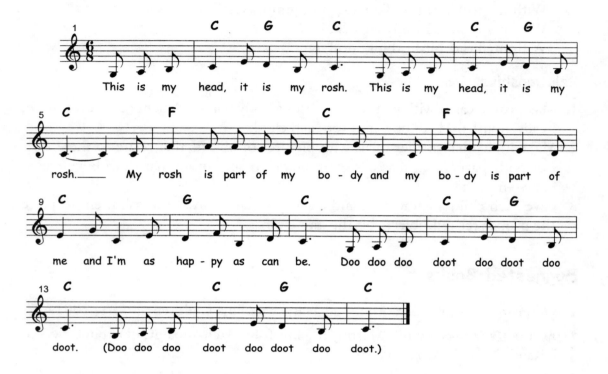

Repeat song, adding another body part each time:

eye - ayin
nose - af
mouth - peh
ear - ozen
hand - yad
leg - regel

Before measure 8, "zip in" the additional body parts using the tune in measures 6-7, then continue with the rest of the song.

Days of the Week

♪♪♪♪♪♪♪♪♪♪♪♪♪♪♪♪♪♪

Objectives

- To teach children the names of the days of the week in English and in Hebrew.
- To discuss things that happen on each day as they relate to the classroom and at home.

Comments

The more children know about what is going to happen during their day, the more comfortable they are. It is important to establish a routine so they know what to expect on any given day. By learning the days of the week and what is particular to each day, children will become more secure about their surroundings and daily activities.

Ideas

Daily Timeline

Create a movable timeline in your classroom that children can easily see and understand. Here are two suggestions:

1. Clothesline daily schedule: String a length of cord or rope from one part of the classroom to another above the heads of the children. Find pictures or clip art

of daily activities, laminate them, and clip them to the cord with clothespins in the order in which the activities happen during the day. You can easily change activities from one day to another, and the reminder of what comes next is always visible.

2. Velcro board schedule: On a large piece of poster board, place pictures of daily classroom activities in order from top to bottom. Put a small piece of Velcro on each picture and the matching side of Velcro on the poster board to attach. You can change the activities as needed. You may also want to write what each activity is next to each picture (e.g., Welcome, Weather, Sharing, Outside Play, Clean Up, Snack, Art Project, Clean Up, Nap).

Display

Somewhere in the classroom creatively display the names of the days of the week in English and in Hebrew as a constant reminder and to use as a teaching tool.

Matching Game

To help children learn the English or Hebrew names for the days of the week:

1. Create game cards with the names of the days of the week written on them. Make one card for each child.
2. Type or write the names of each day of the week in English or Hebrew on small slips of paper and cut them out. You may want to laminate them or cover with clear contact paper to make them last longer. Do one set for each child, and give each child a set. At the same time make a master set on large index cards for yourself.
3. Hold up your large card with the name of one day of the week on it.
4. Children must find the matching word from their slips of paper and place it on their game card.

Suggested Book

One Lighthouse, One Moon, by Anita Lobel. Fairfield, N.J.: Greenwillow, 2000.

Days of the Week

Music & Lyrics: Genevieve Shorr-Hain
& Judy Caplan Ginsburgh

There are sev - en days in ev - ery week.

One two three four five six sev - en. Sev - en days in

ev - ery week. Can you name___ them with me?

Yom Ri - shon *(Sunday),* Yom Shei - ni, *(Monday),* Yom Sh' - li - shi *(Tuesday),*

Yom R' - vi - i *(Wednesday),* Yom Cha - mi - shi *(Thursday),* Yom Shi - shi *(Friday),*

Yom Sha - bat, the days___ of the week.

Dance of the Months

♫♫♫♫♫♫♫♫♫♫♫♫♫♫♫♫

Objective

- To teach the names of the months in Hebrew or in English through a fun dancing game.

Comments

You can substitute any month (Hebrew or English) into this song. This is a good song to sing at the beginning of each new month to introduce the new month or the concept of *Rosh Chodesh* (new month) to the children.

Ideas

Calendar

Display a Hebrew and an English calendar in the classroom. Be sure to include special events, holidays, and birthdays.

Dance

1. Have children form a circle.
2. Give each child a card with the name of a Jewish month on it.

3. Have children walk in a circle singing the first part of the "Dance of the Months."

4. On the instrumental bridge, announce the name of the month, and have the child with that card come to the center of the circle.

5. The other children continue walking around the "chosen month" by singing the second part of the song.

6. After you sing the song, sit and talk about the various things that will happen during that month (e.g., holidays, special field trips). You could even ask the child who has the chosen month to answer first.

Wall-Hanging Calendar

1. Buy a piece of muslin fabric approximately eleven by seventeen inches in size. Either cut the edges with pinking sheers or iron them down with binding tape so they won't ravel.

2. Wrap one eleven-inch end of the fabric rectangle around a wooden dowel. Either glue or sew the edge down around the dowel.

3. With a marker, write the names of the Hebrew months down the right side of the "calendar."

4. Cut a piece of string, and with thumbtacks attach each end to the ends of the dowel. Adjust the length of the string based on where you want to hang the calendar in the room.

5. Cut out pictures of symbols representing various Jewish holidays. You may use greeting cards or stick stickers on cardboard and then cut them out. If you use pictures from magazines or catalogs, glue them to a piece of index stock first, and then cut them out.

6. Stick a tiny piece of Velcro on the back of each holiday picture. Stick the other side of the Velcro onto the wall hanging, placing about four to five pieces in line with each month.

7. At the bottom left corner of the wall hanging, you can glue or stitch a little pocket to hold all of the pictures.

8. As each new Hebrew month begins, ask children to find the pictures representing things that will happen during that month and place them on the wall hanging.

You can also do this using a sheet of "Easy Felt" instead of muslin. Easy Felt is stiffer than regular felt and much easier to cut. Punch a hole on either end of the top long edge of the felt. Insert a pipe cleaner into each hole and secure by twisting it around itself a few times. Then twist the two pipe cleaners together in the middle to form a hanger. Cut shapes of holiday objects out of colorful Easy Felt. Follow the same directions as with the muslin.

Suggested Book

One Lighthouse, One Moon, by Anita Lobel. Fairfield, N.J.: Greenwillow, 2000.

Dance of the Months

Music & Lyrics: "Miss Jackie" Silberg

We are walk-ing in a cir-cle, we are mov-ing to the beat.

Now it's time for ev'-ry one to meet. one to meet.

Tish-rei Tish-rei, we're glad you're here. You're so im-port-ant

to the year. to the year.

Rest of the months:

Cheshvan
Kislev
Tevet
Sh'vat
Adar (I, II)
Nisan
Iyar
Sivan
Tamuz
Av
Elul

Four Seasons

Objectives

- To teach the children about the different seasons of the year and various weather conditions.
- To familiarize them with the names of the seasons in Hebrew and in English.

Comments

In some parts of the world, there are not four distinct seasons, and so children may not be able to experience all of them firsthand. It is still useful to talk about each season and relate them to holidays and activities that happen during them.

(Ba)s'tav—(in the) fall/autumn
(Ba)choref—(in the) winter
(Ba)aviv—(in the) spring
(Ba)kayitz—(in the) summer

Ideas

Season Quiz

Ask children to name special things that happen during each season. They can even draw or cut out pictures to illustrate. Examples:

Summer—hot, sunny, no school, vacation.
Fall—leaves fall off the trees, windy.
Winter—cold, snow, not as many things grow, Chanukah.
Spring—flowers, windy, warmer, Pesach.

Make a Season Collage

1. On a piece of card stock paper, draw two lines, one vertical and one horizontal, to divide the page into quarters.
2. Write the name of a season at the top of each quarter.
3. Give each child a "season grid" and pieces of tissue paper, construction paper, stickers, confetti, and other flat art materials. Ask them to include a tree in each square and decorate it for each season. Provide each child with four precut "tree trunks" and branches of various sizes.
4. Ask students to create a small collage in each square for each season, using the materials provided for leaves and fruit, snow, etc. You can even buy leaf-shaped confetti.

Or: Go outside during each season and collect nature items. Give each child a piece of mat board. Have them glue the nature objects to the mat board. Punch a hole in the top, put a piece of yarn or string through the hole, and hang.

Season Bingo

1. Make bingo cards with the names of the four seasons at the top. You will have four columns across and three to five rows depending upon how many pictures you can find. Make enough cards for each child to have one. You may also want to include the Hebrew words for each season both in Hebrew letters and transliterated English on the cards.
2. Glue photos/pictures/stickers of various seasonal things *randomly* on the cards under the proper season column in which they might occur (examples: wind, flowers, sun, snow, rain, clouds, bare trees, trees with fruit, evergreens, animals, acorns, beach, warm clothes, bathing suit, pile of leaves, rake, snow shovel, fireplace, swimming equipment, trees budding). Be sure to keep a master list of all the items.
3. Call out items, and have children put markers on their cards as they find the items. Play as you would any other bingo game.

Thermometer

1. On a piece of poster board, draw a thermometer with temperature degrees along one side of it.
2. On the side opposite the temperature degrees, glue pictures of types of clothing that would be worn in hot or cold temperatures.

3. Laminate it.
4. Put a small strip of Velcro vertically down the center of the thermometer.
5. Make a small red rectangle, laminate it, and fasten corresponding Velcro to the back of it.
6. As you check the weather, move the red rectangle to an appropriate place on the thermometer to indicate the current temperature.

Suggested Books

The God Around Us, vols. 1 and 2, by Mira Brichto, illustrated by Selina Alko. New York: UAHC Press, 2000, 2001.

Spring Song, by Barbara Seuling, illustrated by Gary Newbold. Orlando, Fla.: Harcourt, 2001.

Fall Is Not Easy, illustrated by Marty Kelley. Middleton, Wisc.: Zino Press Childrens Books, 1998.

Snow, by Uri Shulevitz. New York: Farrar, Straus and Giroux, 1998.

How a Seed Grows, by Helene J. Jordan, illustrated by Loretta Krupinski. New York: Harper Trophy, 1992.

Cap, Hat, Socks and Mittens: A Book About the Four Seasons, by Louise Bordon, illustrated by Lillian Hoban. New York: Scholastic Trade, 1992.

Four Seasons

Music & Lyrics: Judy Caplan Ginsburgh

I See a Mezuzah

♪♪♪♪♪♪♪♪♪♪♪♪♪♪♪♪♪♪

Objective

- To teach children about the mezuzah.

Comments

Children will have many questions about the mezuzah. (Examples: What is it? Why do we put it on our doors, and what doors do we put it on? How should we put it on our doors? What is inside of the mezuzah? Why do they all look different?) The word *mezuzah* literally means "doorpost." Often people "kiss" the mezuzah when they enter a room. To "kiss" the mezuzah, touch the mezuzah with your fingertips, then touch your fingertips to your lips. When a mezuzah is put up on a door, a special prayer is said:

בָּרוּךְ אַתָּה יי אֱלֹהֵינוּ מֶלֶךְ הָעוֹלָם,

אֲשֶׁר קִדְּשָׁנוּ בְּמִצְוֹתָיו וְצִוָּנוּ לִקְבּוֹעַ מְזוּזָה.

    Baruch atah Adonai, Eloheinu Melech haolam, asher kid'shanu b'mitzvotav v'tzivanu likboa mezuzah.

    Praised are You, *Adonai* our God, Creator of the universe, who has sanctified us with mitzvot and commands us to affix the mezuzah.

Ideas

Look at different mezuzahs either around your school or synagogue or in Judaica catalogs. Talk about the different materials that they are made from. Talk about the different shapes and sizes. They may look different, but every mezuzah has the same prayer inside. It contains the first two paragraphs of the *Sh'ma:* "You shall write them upon the doorposts of your house and upon your gates. . . ." This is why we put a mezuzah on our doors—to remind us that we are in a Jewish place and that we should study God's commandments and live by them. A mezuzah should be hung on the right side of the door as you enter the room, and the upper part of the mezuzah should tilt toward the room.

Make an Easy Mezuzah

1. At a hobby store, look for small rectangular plastic containers with plastic stoppers or empty plastic rectangular pencil lead containers. Provide one for each child. Copy the *Sh'ma* prayer on small pieces of paper, one for each child.
2. Remove the stopper, and insert the *Sh'ma* prayer inside the plastic tube. Replace the stopper.
3. Decorate the plastic tube.
4. Glue the tube to a wide craft stick (these come in lots of colors) so it can be nailed to a doorpost.

Suggested Book

A Trip to Mezuzah Land, by Sara Lieberman and Chana Colish. Brooklyn: Merkos Linyonei Chinuch, 1988.

I See a Mezuzah

Music & Lyrics: Sherrie Stohl

Additional lyrics:

2.   When I come to the door of a synagogue,
     I see a mezuzah ...

3.   When I come to the door of my Bubbie's (Zaydie's) house,
     I see a mezuzah ...

The Torah

♪♪♪♪♪♪♪♪♪♪♪♪♪♪♪♪♪♪♪

Objectives

- To know what the Torah looks like and where it "lives."
- To learn respect for the Torah and what it means to us.

Comments

This song provides a great opportunity for your rabbi or cantor to take the children into the synagogue to see the *Aron Kodesh* (Holy Ark) and the Torah contained inside. It can be a time to remind the children about synagogue behavior and respect for the sanctuary and the Torah. Torah scrolls are all handwritten on pieces of parchment by scribes. The pieces of parchment are stitched together. There is no way to erase a mistake. If the scribe makes a mistake, the whole panel must be done over again.

Ideas

Experience the Torah

1. See the Torah: Notice the crowns, the mantle (covering), the *yad* (pointer), the breastplate, the rollers, and the parchment. Ask children to describe how these objects look in their own words (pretty, shiny, old, etc.).

2. Touch the Torah: Let children touch the various ornaments on the Torah and the scroll itself. Explain to them that they cannot touch the letters because the oil from their fingers might smudge them. Ask them to describe how these objects felt in their own words (soft, cold, heavy, etc.).
3. Hear the Torah: Ask the rabbi or cantor to read from the Torah. Ask children to describe how it felt to hear the Torah being read.

Edible Torah

1. Give each child two long pretzel logs, a fruit roll, and a skinny piece of licorice.
2. Have children unroll the fruit roll on pieces of wax paper. Place a pretzel log at each end of the fruit roll, and roll both ends toward the center. Tie together with the licorice (or the long coiled brand of fruit rolls).

Huggable Torah

For each Torah:

1. Stuff two old knee-high stockings with cotton stuffing.
2. Tie at the top when desired height is reached, and pull the excess stocking back down over the stuffed part.
3. With thread or string, tie each stocking near the top and the bottom.
4. Give each child a rectangular piece of fabric or felt that will be large enough to wrap around the center of the stuffed Torah as a mantle. Have them decorate it.
5. Wrap the mantle around the Torah and glue to secure.
6. Children will each have their very own soft Torah to use in the classroom or take home.

Suggested Books

Hello, Hello, Are You There God? by Molly Cone, illustrated by Rosalind Charney Kaye. New York: UAHC Press, 1999.

A Child's Garden of Torah: A Read Aloud Bedtime Bible, by Joel Lurie Grishaver. Los Angeles: Torah Aura, 1998.

The Torah

Music & Lyrics: Sherrie Stohl

The To-rah sits in-side the ark, it waits for us each day. It feels so good to have it near, when we come to pray. It feels so good to have it near, when we come to pray. Oh, thank you God for this spe-cial gift you've giv-en to light our way. Thank you God for the To-rah to guide us ev-ery day.

S'lichah, Todah, B'vakashah

Objective

- To teach the pronunciation and meaning of the Hebrew words *s'lichah* (I'm sorry), *todah* (thank you), and *b'vakashah* (please).

Comments

Children should become comfortable using "manners" words both in Hebrew and English when appropriate. These words are not easy to pronounce, but singing them will make it easier. *S'lichah* also means "Excuse me"; *b'vakashah* also means "You are welcome."

Ideas

What's Polite?

Give children various situations where they might need to use one of these words, and have them discuss or act out the situation and what they should do. (Example: One of you is building a house out of blocks. Someone else runs through the class and accidentally knocks your house down. What should the careless person say?)

Manners Game

1. Take an empty half-pint milk carton. Flatten the top and tape it down. You should now have a square cube, which will serve as a die.
2. Cut out six pictures from magazines of people of different ages in a variety of situations that might suggest a story (examples: two people waving, someone carrying packages, a person in a wheelchair, a child eating cotton candy, etc.). Glue one picture on each side of the die.
3. Ask children to take turns rolling the milk-carton die. When it lands on a picture they must try to think of a helpful phrase or story that fits the picture rolled. (Examples: "Hi, it's nice to meet you," "Can I help you?," "I have enjoyed being with you today," "Thanks for the treat!")

Suggested Books

Manners, by Aliki. Canada: Mulberry Books, 1997.

The Grouchy Ladybug, by Eric Carle. Glenview, Ill: Scott Foresman, 1996.

S'lichah, Todah, B'vakashah

Music & Lyrics: Judy Caplan Ginsburgh

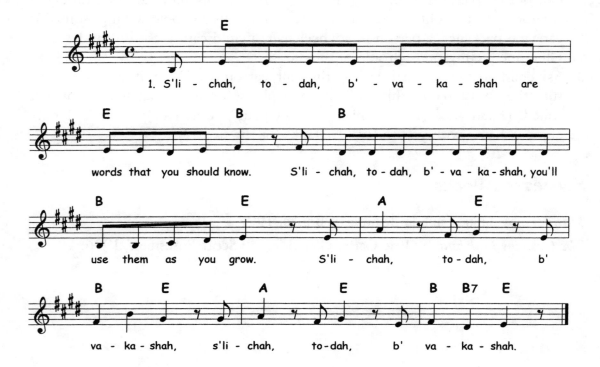

1. S'li - chah, to - dah, b' - va - ka - shah are words that you should know. S'li - chah, to - dah, b' - va - ka - shah, you'll use them as you grow. S'li - chah, to - dah, b' va - ka - shah, s'li - chah, to-dah, b' va - ka - shah.

Additional lyrics:

2. S'lichah means I'm sorry.
   It's a word that you should know.
   S'lichah means I'm sorry.
   You'll use it as you grow.

3. Todah means thank you ...

4. B'vakashah means please ...

One Balloon, Two Balloons

♪♪♪♪♪♪♪♪♪♪♪♪♪♪♪♪♪

Objectives

- To teach children how to count to ten in English and in Hebrew.
- To encourage early math skills.

Comments

This song can provide the foundation for learning early math skills. Always look for opportunities to use math terms in the classroom. (Examples: "Hannah has a *square* block, and Aaron has a *rectangle*"; "Jonathan is *first* in line, Ari is *second,* Anna is *third,* and Rebecca is *last*"; count the number of doors you pass as you walk down the hall; ask children to select and count out a specified number of crayons to use before beginning an art project.)

Have children hold up the appropriate number of fingers as the song is sung. Do this for both the English and the Hebrew parts of the song. The Hebrew part of the song may be a bit difficult for most young children to sing along with, but they can count with their fingers as each new number is sung.

Ideas

Classroom Inventory

1. Make classroom inventory cards by cutting pictures out of magazines of items that may or may not be found in your classroom (examples: blocks, balls, table, chair, truck, window, door, elephant, bathtub).

2. Glue the pictures on cards. Underneath each picture write the name of the object. Laminate the cards.
3. Hold up a card, and ask children to look around the room and count the number of each item that they see in the classroom. Including some cards with things that are not found in the room (e.g., bathtub) allows them to learn the number zero also. (They can either say the number, show you the number with their fingers, or write the number.)

Visuals

Post a chart somewhere in the room with the numbers one through ten in English and in Hebrew.

Matching Game

Cut out balloon shapes using construction paper, foam, or felt. Number some of them from one to ten. Place dots on others ranging from one to ten dots. Children must match a numbered balloon with the appropriate number of dots on another balloon.

Suggested Books

Let's Count, by Tana Hoban. Fairfield, N.J.: Greenwillow, 1999.

Ten Little Ladybugs, by Melanie Gerth, illustrated by Laura Huliska-Beith. Santa Monica, Calif.: Piggy Toes Press, 2001.

Hippos Go Berserk, by Sandra Boynton. New York: Little Simon, 2000.

Counting Kisses, by Karen Katz. New York: Margaret McElderry, 2001.

One, Two, Three to the Zoo, by Eric Carle. New York: Putnam Publishing Group, 1998.

Turtle Splash, by Cathryn Falwell. Fairfield, N.J.: Greenwillow, 2001.

One Balloon, Two Balloons

Music & Lyrics: Shai Specht

One bal-loon, two bal-loons, three bal-loons and four, five bal-loons, six bal-loons,

sev-en bal-loons and more, eight bal-loons, nine bal-loons, ten bal-loons and then

Let's start count-ing bal-loons a-gain. Ba-

lon e-chad, sh'nei ba-lo-nim, sh'-lo-shah ba-lo-nim, ar-ba-ah, cha-mi-

shah ba-lo-nim, shi-shah ba-lo-nim, shiv'-ah ba-lo-nim, sh'mo-nah, tish'-

ah ba-lo-nim, v'-a-sa-rah ba-lo-nim. Let's start count-ing bal-

loons a-gain. We've had fun count-ing bal-loons, my friend.

A Line Needs a Leader

♪♪♪♪♪♪♪♪♪♪♪♪♪♪♪♪♪

Objectives

- To help children understand the concept of walking down the hall in an orderly fashion.
- To let them know that every space in the line is important.

Comments

This is a terrific song to sing or play as you walk down the hall in a line. The words are so descriptive and should make everyone feel good about their place in the line. One thing that will help children initially learn to stay in line is to take a long length of rope and tie handles (loops) on it every twelve inches or so. Make a loop for each child. When the children are in line, give them each a handle on the rope to hold as they walk down the hall.

Ideas

Number Line

1. Make a visible line where children will line up when they have to leave the room as a group by cutting out various shapes of various colors.
2. Put a large number on each shape.

3. Laminate each shape, and tape them in numerical order to the floor, making sure there are enough for each child to stand on one.
4. Children will stand on a designated numbered shape as they line up.
5. To encourage children to line up quickly and quietly, you can let them know that whenever they are each on their own numbered shape, they will be rewarded by having you randomly select a number out of a container. Whoever is on that number gets a small prize.

A Line Needs a Leader

Music & Lyrics: Billy B.

Well__ a line needs a lead-er, it needs a ca-boose. It

needs to be straight__ and it needs to be loose. Don't__

push, don't__ shove, just take your time and you walk, walk,

walk in your line. Yeah,__ you walk, (don't talk) walk in your line. The

whole class has to go from here__ to there.__ The tea-cher has to know

just who's where. So some-bod-y's first__ and some-bod-y's last and

in be-tween__ you got the rest of the class.

walk in your line. Leave___ a lit - tle space in front and a

lit - tle be - hind. Yeah, you walk walk in your line.

* In this section the following words may be substituted:

If you cut in, people get pushed.
When you cut in, people get squashed.
People say, "Hey, you have to go to the back.
I was here first and that's a fact."

Rub-A-Dub-Dub
(Wash Your Hands)

♪♪♪♪♪♪♪♪♪♪♪♪♪♪♪♪♪

Objective

* To teach children about cleanliness and the importance of washing their hands, especially before they eat.

Comments

This song is one that is probably better to listen to than to try to sing with. However, the children will have fun singing along on the "rub-a-dub-dub" part. The song says a lot about keeping clean and staying healthy in a fun way. In traditional Jewish law, a person must wash his or her hands ritually before eating a meal at which bread is served. The origin of the law is biblical and can be found in Exodus 30:17–21. Here, Moses is commanded to make a copper vessel and to place it at the entrance to the altar area so the priests could wash their hands before making sacrifices at the altar. There are two reasons given for the need to wash the hands. One is cleanliness. The other is to make the hands pure before performing a ritual act. After the Temple was destroyed in 70 C.E., the table in the home came to represent the Temple altar. The bread placed on it came to symbolize the offerings that were once brought to the priests. The blessing we say for washing hands is:

בָּרוּךְ אַתָּה יהוה אֱלֹהֵינוּ מֶלֶךְ הָעוֹלָם,
אֲשֶׁר קִדְּשָׁנוּ בְּמִצְוֹתָיו וְצִוָּנוּ עַל נְטִילַת יָדָיִם.

Baruch atah Adonai, Eloheinu Melech haolam, asher kid'shanu b'mitzvotav v'tzivanu al n'tilat yadayim.

Praised are You, Adonai our God, Creator of the universe, who has sanctified us with Your commandments and has commanded us to wash our hands.

Please note: The ritual of hand washing is not actually meant to clean hands, but rather to make them ritually pure or ready to participate in a ritual. This subtlety will most likely be lost on the students; however, it is an important distinction and may come up in conversation with parents or other teachers.

Ideas

Pied Piper

This activity will make it more fun for children to wash their hands and will help facilitate a smooth transition to the hand-washing area.

When it is time for everyone to wash their hands, you or a designated "pied piper" student should blow bubbles as you lead the way. You may want to use a very small bubble container like the ones used for weddings and refill the container as needed. When the children see the bubbles, they will know it is time to wash their hands. You may have to have some instructional bubble blowing lessons initially if students are going to blow the bubbles. You can also cut out some soap bubbles or water drips that have been drawn on heavy paper. Laminate them and stick them on the floor, making a path to the sink or hand-washing area. Children must step on the bubbles as they go to wash their hands.

What's the Soap?

Make washing hands fun by providing a variety of different kinds of soaps and paper towels. Use soaps in different colors and scents, foam soap, and soap flakes. Buy some pretty paper hand towels or fun paper towels.

Suggested Books

Wash Your Hands, by Tony Ross. La Jolla, Calif.: Kane/Miller Book Publishers, 2000.

Dirty Little Boy, by Margaret Wise Brown, illustrated by Steven Salerno. New York: Winslow Press, 2001.

Rub-A-Dub-Dub

Music & Lyrics: Dean Friedman

1. Oh wash your hands be-fore you eat.___
Scrub them good and take your seat.___ 'Cause if you eat with dirt-y hands___ those
germs will make their nas-ty plans.___ So rub-a-dub-dub, (rub-a-dub-dub)
wash and scrub. (wash and scrub) You can't see them but germs are real so
wash your hands___ be-fore ev-ery meal.

Additional verses:

2. Those invisible germs will wiggle and slide,
They'll squish and squirm as they crawl inside.
They'll do their dirty work so quick.
They'll make you ill, they'll make you sick.
So, rub-a-dub-dub …

3. So grab a great big bar of soap,
Wash those hands, don't be a dope.
Those slimy germs are ugly and mean
But they can't get you if your hands are clean.
So, rub-a-dub-dub …

B'tei-avon

♪♪♪♪♪♪♪♪♪♪♪♪♪♪♪♪♪♪

Objectives

- To teach that the word *b'tei-avon* means "enjoy your meal."
- To teach the *HaMotzi* blessing.

Comments

Getting into the habit of saying the *HaMotzi* blessing before eating is a good thing to do. Hopefully the children will take this classroom tradition home to implement there as well. In Jewish tradition, no food is more important than bread. It is for this reason that when the blessing over the bread is recited before a meal, it covers all foods to be eaten during the meal.

בָּרוּךְ אַתָּה יי אֱלֹהֵינוּ מֶלֶךְ הָעוֹלָם,

הַמּוֹצִיא לֶחֶם מִן הָאָרֶץ.

Baruch atah Adonai, Eloheinu Melech haolam, hamotzi lechem min haaretz.
Praised are You, Adonai our God, Creator of the universe, who brings forth bread from the earth.

Ideas

Challah Treat

Purchase some "canned" breadstick dough. Open the can and separate the individual breadsticks. Place three breadsticks for each child on pieces of wax paper. Teach children to braid the three pieces of dough to make a challah. Make sure you press each end of each challah so that the three strands fuse firmly together. Spray the tops with butter spray. Place on greased baking pans, and bake as per instructions on the package. When the challahs are cool, wrap them decoratively and send them home with the *HaMotzi* prayer attached.

Color Plate

Provide a variety of healthy snacks on a tray. Make enough for each child to have one of each. The goal is for the children to fill their plates with one snack from every color group. (Here are some ideas: Orange—carrot, yellow—cheese, green—sliced pickle or cucumber, white—cracker, black—raisin, red—tomato or pepper slice, etc.)

Discuss what they should select for each color, and then let the children put their plates together.

Huggable Happy Challah

1. Stuff three knee-high stockings with cotton stuffing.
2. Tie each one at the top, and then tie the three tops together.
3. Assist children in braiding the three stockings like a challah, and tie the three ends together at the bottom.
4. Children can cut eyes, mouth, and so on from stick-on felt to decorate.

Suggested Books

Lunch, by Denise Fleming. New York: Henry Holt, 1998.

Eating the Alphabet: Fruits and Vegetables from A–Z, by Lois Ehlert. New York: Red Wagon, 1996.

The God Around Us: Volume 2: The Valley of Blessings, by Mira Brichto, illustrated by Selina Alko. New York: UAHC Press, 2001.

B'tei-avon

Music & Lyrics: Genevieve Shorr-Hain
& Judy Caplan Ginsburgh

It's time for snack, come a-long. Let's sit down, ev'-ry-one.

Let's eat snack, come a-long. Ummm! Yum! B'-tei-a - von. Ba-

ruch A - tah, A - do-nai___ E - lo - hei - nu, Me-lech ha - o - lam, ha -

mo - tzi le - chem min ha - a - retz. We give thanks to God for bread. We

qui-et-ly take a seat, drink our juice and have a bite to eat. We

have our nap - kins in our laps. Let's eat. B'-tei-a - von. Let's

eat. B'-tei-a - von. Let's eat. B'-tei-a - von.___

Tot Birkat HaMazon

♫♫♫♫♫♫♫♫♫♫♫♫♫♫♫♫♫♫

Objective

• To introduce children to the *Birkat HaMazon* blessing, which may lead to discussions of some children who do not have a lot to eat.

Comments

This song uses part of the actual tune from *Birkat HaMazon*. It is a great introduction for children so they will have some recognition of the tune when they are older and learn more of it.

בָּרוּךְ אַתָּה יי הַזָּן אֶת־הַכֹּל.

Baruch atah Adonai, Eloheinu Melech haolam, hazan et hakol.
Praised are You, Adonai our God, Source of food for all.

Ideas

What Do Others Eat?

Look at a globe or a map of the world. Talk about what children eat in other countries. If you have parents from other cultures, ask if they can bring a traditional dish in for the class to sample.

Placemats

Make placemats by using a large rectangular piece of construction paper or index stock paper. Give each child a copy of the portion of the *Birkat HaMazon* that is sung in the song. Have them glue this in the center of the rectangle. On the rest of the placemat, glue pictures of foods they like to eat. Laminate and use as placemats for snack.

Suggested Books

Bread Is for Eating, by David and Phyllis Gershator, illustrated by Emma Shaw-Smith. New York: Henry Holt, 1998.

Everybody Bakes Bread, by Norah Dooley, illustrated by Peter J. Thornton. Minneapolis: Carolrhoda Books, 1996.

Tot Birkat HaMazon

Music & Lyrics: Anita Schubert
(based on traditional melody)

Ba - ruch A - tah,___ A - do - nai, ha - zan___ et ha - kol.

We give thanks to A - do - nai for fill - ing up our bowls.

Thank You for the land that gives us such good food. Bless us all with peace, and

won't You please in - clude all of Yis - ra - eil and ev' - ry - one on earth.

You've been good to us since birth. Help us build a bet - ter

world to feed,___ one and all. Ba - ruch A - tah,___ A - do -

nai, ha - zan___ et ha - kol.

* The middle section of this song is not sung on the recording. We felt that
this abbreviated version might easily become a standard in your classrooms,
easy enough for young children to sing each day after snack or a meal.
We wanted to also provide you with the entire song as written by the author.

Colors in My World

♪♪♪♪♪♪♪♪♪♪♪♪♪♪♪♪♪♪♪

Objective

- To teach children some basic colors in Hebrew and in English.

Comments

Feel free to sing the song and add other colors in English or in Hebrew.

Ideas

Color Snack

Use a few drops of food coloring in cream cheese to make different colors. Put each color in a different container. Using craft sticks, have children spread various colors of cream cheese on mini-bagels. Have them decorate with raisins, sunflower seeds, chocolate chips, etc., and then eat as a snack.

Color Sorting

Cut a square of white tagboard. On it glue smaller squares of construction paper in nine different colors. When finished, it should look similar to a tic-tac-toe board. Give children objects to sort by colors such as crayons, buttons, teddy bear markers, chips, etc. Have them sort them to the proper color on the sorting card.

How Many Colors Can You Find?

Ask children to name foods, objects, and so on that are the various colors you are studying (example: red—fire truck, pizza sauce, ketchup, tomato). Have them go home and find at least five things from each of the colors in the song at their house. Have them make a list with their parent(s) to bring to school to share.

Monochromatic Color Collage

1. Make sure you have lots of crayon shavings (take discarded crayons and sharpen or grate them to get shavings) in various shades of all of the primary colors.
2. Have each child select one color and its shades from the crayon shavings and arrange them on a piece of wax paper.
3. Once the shavings are arranged, place another piece of waxed paper over the first, trapping the shavings in between the two.
4. Carefully move the collage to a place where you can iron the two pieces to one another to seal.
5. Cut out construction paper or mat board frames in corresponding colors (make two frame cutouts for each collage).
6. Tape or glue the frame to the front and back of the collage.

Color Concentration

1. On a piece of poster board, glue twelve library pockets, four across and three down.
2. Number each pocket at the bottom from one through twelve.
3. Laminate the entire poster.
4. Cut a slit at the top of each library pocket so you can insert a card.
5. Take some index cards, and on one side write the name of a color. On another card, paint or color a spot of that same color. Make six sets of cards using colors you are learning about.
6. Place the cards face down randomly into the pockets.
7. Ask a child to guess two numbers. When you pull the cards out of the selected pockets, if they match, that team gets a point. If they do not match, the cards go back to their original pockets. A good memory will help. You can also substitute Hebrew names of colors.

Suncatchers

1. Precut shapes from clear contact paper (do not peel the backing off yet). Each student will need two matching shapes.
2. Peel the backing off of one of each student's shapes. Have them carefully decorate the sticky side of the shape with Jewish-themed confetti or glitter. Talk

about the different colors as they decorate.

3. Carefully peel the backing off of the second shape, and place the sticky sides together.

4. Punch a hole at the top of each shape, and make a hanging loop with a pipe cleaner or yarn.

Suggested Books

The Color Kittens, by Margaret Wise Brown and Alice Provensen, illustrated by Martin Provensen. Westminster, Md.: Golden Books Publishing, 2000.

Colors, by Robert Crowther. Cambridge, Mass.: Candlewick Press, 2001.

Colors in My World

Music & Lyrics: Judy Caplan Ginsburgh

1. There are col-ors all a-round, col-ors like a rain-bow, lots of col-ors in my world. There are col-ors all a-round, col-ors like a rain-bow, lots of col-ors in my world. There's ka-chol (blue) for the sky where the birds fly way up high. There's ka-chol (blue) for the sky, lots of col-ors in my world.

Additional verses:

2. There's tzahov (yellow) for the sun. When it shines we play and have fun.
   There's tzahov (yellow) for the sun. Lots of colors in my world.

3. There's yarok (green) for the grass where we really shouldn't throw trash.
   There's yarok (green) for the grass. Lots of colors in my world.

4. There's adom (red) for the flowers. They grow tall when the rain showers.
   There's adom (red) for the flowers. Lots of colors in my world.

Opposite Blues

Objective

- To teach opposites.

Comments

Feel free to add any other opposites you wish to this song.

Ideas

Collection

Collect objects around the classroom that are small and large, hard and soft, etc. Have children sort them into categories.

Simon Says

Play "Simon says" with opposite concepts: "Simon says reach high/low; walk loudly/softly; come near/go far," etc.

Photo Opposites

Take pictures of opposites or find them in magazines (e.g., plate full/plate empty; one child near camera/one far; going up steps/going down; brick/feathers). Put them in a book and label each opposite pair.

Scarf/Streamer Opposites

Give each child a scarf or a streamer. Ask them to wave the scarf or streamer in certain ways that indicate opposites: high/low, up/down, fast/slow, heavy/light, etc.

Suggested Books

Olivia Owl's Opposites, by Maurice Pledger. San Diego: Silver Dolphin, 2001.

Hot, Cold, Shy, Bold, by Pamela Harris. Tonawanda, N.Y.: Kids Can Press, 1998.

Opposites, by Sandra Boynton. New York: Little Simon, 1995.

Let's Find Opposites with Bob the Builder, by Jenny Miglis, illustrated by Vince Giorrano. New York: Simon Spotlight, 2002.

Night/Day: A Book of Eye-Catching Opposites, edited by M. Tingley, illustrated by Herve Tullet. New York: Little Brown, 1999.

Opposite Blues

Music & Lyrics: Vincent

Additional verses:

2. I'll be big and I'll be small …

3. I'll be noisy and I'll be quiet …

4. I will frown and then I'll smile …

Tzedakah

♪♪♪♪♪♪♪♪♪♪♪♪♪♪♪♪♪♪♪

Objective

- To teach children the meaning of *tzedakah*.

Comments

Children should be taught that giving money is not the only way we can give *tzedakah*. *Tzedakah* can also be a kind word, food, toys, and so on.

Ideas

Decoupage *Tzedakah* Box

Ask each child to bring in an empty juice can with a plastic lid. Place stickers or pictures of Jewish symbols from catalogs, magazines, or old holiday cards on the can with glue. Feel free to overlap pictures and cover the entire can. Once cans are covered, spray with varnish outside and let dry. Cut a slit in the lid and put on top.

Tzedakah in Action

1. If you have a senior group that meets or resides near your preschool, bring the children to visit with them or sing for them. Make cards and leave them at a retirement home.

2. Ask each child to bring in a lightly used toy or game of theirs to give to a child who does not have as much. Donate them to a homeless shelter in your area.
3. Ask children to bring a can of food to be donated to a food bank in your area.
4. Collect *tzedakah* each Friday at school. Keep track of how much money has been collected so the children can watch the amount grow as the year goes on. At the end of the year, choose several charities (either local or more global) to present to the children. Explain them and what they do to help others. Let children choose where they want the money to go. If they choose more than one, this is a great math moment where you can use a pie chart to illustrate how much will go to each charity.

Suggested Books

The Giving Box, by Fred Rogers. Philadelphia: Running Press, 2000.

The Very Best Place for A Penny, by Dina Herman Rosenfeld. Brooklyn: Merkos Linyonei Chinuch, 1984.

The Berenstain Bears Think of Those in Need, by Stan and Jan Berenstain. New York: Random House, 1999.

Tzedakah

Music & Lyrics: Judy Caplan Ginsburgh

Share, Share, Share

♪♪♪♪♪♪♪♪♪♪♪♪♪♪♪♪♪

Objective

- To help children learn to "share" and "cooperate" with one another.

Comments

When children come to preschool, it is often the first time they have ever had to play and share with anyone else. Teaching "sharing," "cooperation," and "friendship" are important concepts in the preschool classroom.

Ideas

Cooperative Roll

1. Cut the bottom two to three inches off of two plastic milk jugs (cut under the end of the handle).
2. Paint or decorate the milk jugs. You may also want to put some colorful tape around the edges to smooth them.
3. For an inside activity, have two children sit on the floor across from each other. One will be the "roller," and one will be the "catcher." The roller will roll the ball to the catcher (who has the jug), and they will both try to make it go into

the jug. Have them scoot farther and farther away from each other or use different-sized balls to make it more challenging. They should take turns being "roller" or "catcher."

4. Children can also play together outside by tossing the balls and trying to catch them in the milk jugs.

Note: You can do something similar with hula hoops and bean bags. Have one child hold the hula hoop and another try to toss a bean bag in the middle of it from various distances.

Children will have to share and cooperate in order to play.

Weave a Web of Friendship

1. Have children sit on the floor in a circle. One child is designated as the "spider."
2. The "spider" holds a big ball of yarn. While holding tightly to one end of the yarn, the "spider" rolls the ball to someone else in the circle. As they roll the yarn, they must say something nice to the person they are rolling it to (example: "I like Rachel's glasses").
3. This continues until every child has had a turn to be the "spider" and a web is woven throughout the whole circle. Make sure children hold tightly onto a piece of the yarn before rolling it to someone else, or place a piece of masking tape to hold the yarn before it is rolled to the next "spider." If you tape it, you will be able to save the web and observe its patterns after the children have left the circle.
4. Variation: Have a small group of children (four to five) sit around a piece of poster board. Have them roll the yarn back and forth, and tape the ends to the poster board. Then you can display the web designs that were shared.

Sharing Show and Tell

Ask each child to bring something in for show-and-tell that they can share with the whole class (examples: puzzle, snack, movie, etc.).

Friendship Chain

Give each child a strip of construction paper. Either have them write their name on it or glue a picture of themselves on it. When all are complete, connect them together to make a paper chain symbolizing that everyone in the class is a friend sharing and learning together.

Suggested Books

I Am Sharing, by Mercer Mayer. New York: Random House, 1995.

The Big Brown Box, by Marisabina Russo. Fairfield, N.J.: Greenwillow, 2000.

Little Mouse and the Big Red Apple, by A. H. Benjamin, illustrated by Gwyneth Williamson. Oakland, Calif.: Tiger Tales, 2001.

A Cake All for Me, by Karen Magnuson Beil, illustrated by Paul Meisel. New York: Holiday House, 1998.

Mine: A Sesame Street Book about Sharing, by Linda Hayward, illustrated by Norman Gorbaty. New York: Random House, 1988.

The Doorbell Rang, by Pat Hutchins. Parsippany, N.J.: Pearson Learning, 1989.

Share, Share, Share

Music & Lyrics: Jon & Josh Nelson

1. Well, I was out on the play-ground and I felt like play-ing ball

I went o - ver to the oth - ers but they

would-n't let me play at all. Then a -

long came a teach-er and she told us all some-thing new.

If you share share share, then things will work out for you.

You got - ta share, share, share if you

want things to go your way. You got - ta

share, share, share if you want things to go your way.____ So lis-ten to what I say to you.____ Shar-ing is the on-ly____ thing to do. You got-ta share, share,____ share, and things will work out____ for you.____

2. Well, back in my class I was doing some arts and crafts,
   When the thing I was building came down with a great big crash.
   So I asked my friend if I could share his glue.
   He said, "OK, I'll be happy to share with you!"

I'm So Mad

Objective

- To empower children to express their feelings in positive ways and to teach them ways to have self control.

Comments

This song provides a fun way for children to understand a variety of feelings. As they act them out with the song, they will become less inhibited about expressing their own feelings.

Ideas

Guess the Feeling

Have children act out emotions/feelings with their bodies. Encourage them to use their whole bodies (examples: smile means they are happy; shrugged shoulders and wide eyes means they are confused, etc.). Have other children guess the feeling.

Puppets

Children can make puppets out of a variety of materials, or there are a number of resources that sell puppets that can help express feelings. Ask each child to make four to five different puppets (mad, sad, excited, tired, happy).

Puppets can be made from the following materials:

- Paper plates and craft sticks: draw a face or decorate with buttons, yarn, pasta, etc.
- Old socks: decorate with yarn, sequins, buttons, etc.
- Toilet paper tubes: Decorate with fabric, pipe cleaners, paper, beads, etc. Two fingers can be inserted into the tube.
- Felt: makes finger puppets.
- Clean flyswatter: decorate a face on it.

A table turned on its side can provide an impromptu puppet theater.

Feelings in History

Read various statements from the Bible or books on Jewish history and have children hold up the puppet that expresses how they would feel in each situation (examples: Abraham had to leave his home—sad; Miriam sang and danced when we crossed the Red Sea—happy). Discuss why.

Feeling Murals

Post several large pieces of butcher paper on the wall. Put a different feeling word at the top of each. Have children look for pictures that illustrate each of the feelings. Cut them out and paste them on the appropriate sheet.

Suggested Books

Feelings, by Aliki. Fairfield, N.J.: Greenwillow, 1986.

My Many Colored Days, by Dr. Seuss, illustrated by Steve Johnson and Lou Fancher. New York: Knopf, 1998.

Today I Feel Silly and Other Moods That Make My Day, by Jamie Lee Curtis, illustrated by Laura Cornell. New York: Harper Collins Juvenile Books, 1998.

Glad Monster/Sad Monster: A Book About Feelings, by Anne Miranda, illustrated by Ed Emberley. Boston: Little, Brown, 1997.

The Chocolate Covered Cookie Tantrum, by Deborah Blumenthal, illustrated by Harvey Stephenson. New York: Clarion Books, 1999.

I'm So Mad

Music & Lyrics: "Miss Jackie" Silberg
(extra lyrics by Judy Caplan Ginsburgh)

1. I'm so mad I could scream. I'm so mad I could scream. I'm so mad, I'm real - ly mad, I could scream, I could scream, I could scream.

Additional verses:

2. I'm so sad I could cry ...

3. I'm so excited I could jump ...

4. I'm so tired I could sleep ...

5. I'm so happy I could smile ...

Be a Mensch!

Objectives

- To teach children to say the word "mensch."
- To teach children some of the qualities a mensch has.

Comments

Teaching the qualities of being a mensch can become something that is ongoing in the classroom. Encourage children to "catch" each other doing nice things. Be a role model yourself and praise children who act like a mensch. "Mensch" is actually a Yiddish word, which means "nice person."

Ideas

A Mensch at Home

Ask children to try to do something at home during the week that a "mensch" would do. At the end of the week, ask them to share what they did.

Mensch of the Week

Create a ribbon, crown, certificate, or award button that can be given to a child who has been particularly "mensch-like." Every Friday select a "mensch of the week," and give that child the "award" and some special privileges. Be sure to let the whole class know why that child was named mensch of the week, and send a note home to the parents as well.

Mensch Jar

Decorate a jar or canister, and designate it as the "mensch jar." This will be the place where children or teachers can deposit pictures or written words about mensch-like acts in the classroom. Share them and praise them.

Suggested Book

The Chanukah Blessing, by Peninnah Schram, illustrated by Jeff Allon. New York: UAHC Press, 2001.

Be a Mensch!

Music & Lyrics: Wally Schachet-Briskin

1. What should you do when you hurt some-one?___ What should you do when your play-ing's done?___ How should you act, do you have a clue?___ Just ask your-self what a mensch would do. Be a mensch, (be a mensch) be a mensch. (be a mensch) Think of oth-er peo-ple, be a mensch. Be a mensch, (be a mensch) be a mensch. (be a mensch) Act be-fore you're asked, be a mensch.

(Spoken: Beep beep! Get out of my way! Oops! I should behave like a mensch. Excuse me, could you please let me through? Thank you!)

Additional verses:

2. A mensch is kind, a mensch is polite.
A mensch will always try to do things right.
Act like a mensch, show the best that's in you.
Just ask yourself what a mensch would do.
Be a mensch ...
(Hey, give me that toy! Uh-oh, I know better. What would a mensch do?
Excuse me, may I play with that toy when you're finished? Thanks a lot!)

3. So say you're sorry when you hurt someone.
Put your toys away when your playing's done.
Use your words saying "please" and "thank you".
That is what a mensch would do.
Be a mensch ...

Z'man Lishon

♫♫♫♫♫♫♫♫♫♫♫♫♫♫♫♫♫♫

Objective

- A song to settle the children down for a nap.

Comments

This is a listening song. Hopefully it will have a calming effect and help the children get ready to rest. It is always a good idea to play soft music at the beginning of naptime. Dim the lights, put on the lullabies, and create a naptime mood.

Ideas

Nap Mural

Have children draw or paint a mural to put on the ceiling so they can look up at it during naptime, or stick glow-in-the-dark objects to the ceiling to make naptime more fun.

Dream Pillows

1. Give each child two pieces of Easy Felt.
2. Punch holes all the way around the outer edges of the felt approximately three inches apart. Make sure you have an even number of holes.

3. Let children decorate their pillow with markers.

4. Thread a large plastic craft needle with a double thickness of yarn long enough to stitch around the entire pillow.

5. Teach children to lace the two pieces together by going in one hole and out the other. Start with one of the center holes at the top of the long side of the rectangle. Make sure the first stitch goes down into the hole and back up out of the second hole. Leave a long string of yarn (eight to ten inches) hanging. You may want to tape this to the pillow so the child will not pull it through. You will use this to tie the two ends together when the lacing is finished.

6. Leave a small opening, and have students stuff in some cotton batting before sewing all the way around the pillow. [Some students may be able to do the sewing, or you may need to help them].

7. If you have punched an even number of holes, the last stitch the child makes will come up out of the last hole. In order to secure the end of the yarn, take the strand that came up out of the last hole and the strand from the first hole. Tie these two strands of yarn together in a double knot and then a bow.

Or: Sew (or ask someone else to sew) small (approximately four- by four-inch square) pillows, one for each child. Have children decorate them with permanent markers with their name and nighttime objects like stars and moons. This can be a special pillow that they can snuggle with during naptime.

Suggested Books

Good Night Moon, by Margaret Wise Brown, illustrated by Clement Hurd. New York: Harper Collins Juvenile, 1991 (reissue).

Sleepy Book, by Charlotte Zolotow, illustrated by Stefano Vitale. New York: Harper Collins Juvenile, 2001.

Sleepytime Rhyme, by Remy Charlip. Fairfield, N.J.: Greenwillow, 1999.

Z'man Lishon

Music & Lyrics: Ronit Ben-Arie
(English lyrics by Judy Caplan Ginsburgh)

Zeh z'man li - shon,   zeh z'man li - shon,
It's time to sleep,   it's time to sleep.

ha - cha - lom o - mer sha - lom._____
May your dreams be filled with peace._____

Zeh z'man li - shon,   zeh z'man li - shon,
It's time to sleep,   it's time to sleep.

ha - cha - lom o - mer sha - lom._____
May your dreams be filled with peace._____

Shalom Chaverim

♫♫♫♫♫♫♫♫♫♫♫♫♫♫♫♫♫

Objectives

- To teach children the meaning of *shalom chaverim*.
- To make the transition of going home easier.

Comments

Just as it is sometimes difficult for young children to leave home and come to school, some have so much fun at school that it can also be difficult to leave their friends and go home. This song can help with that transition and can also physically make the transition to move into a carpool line or line up at the door easier too. Remember, when you say *shalom*, you are never really saying good-bye. You can also teach children to say *shalom v'l'hitraot*, which means "good-bye and I will see you later" (or, "until I see you again").

Ideas

Feel free to add these verses:

It's time for us to all go home (2 times)
Now it's time to say *shalom*
Good-bye, our day is done.

84

We'll all come back to school again (2 times)
Now it's time to say *shalom*
Good-bye, our day is done.

Use this verse to get children to line up or leave in an orderly fashion as their name is sung:

Let's say good-bye to Adam now (2 times)
Now it's time to say *shalom*
Good-bye, our day is done.

Shalom Chaveirim

Music & Lyrics: Judy Caplan Ginsburgh
& Genevieve Shorr-Hain

Hebrew/Yiddish Vocabulary Used in Curriculum

Word	Meaning	Song	Page
adom	red	"Colors in My World"	63
af	nose	"My Body Is Part of Me"	22
(ba)aviv	(in the) spring	"Four Seasons"	33
ayin	eye	"My Body Is Part of Me"	22
balon(im)	balloon(s)	"One Balloon, Two Balloons"	45
Birkat HaMazon		"Tot Birkat HaMazon"	59
boker tov	good morning	"Boker Tov Means Good Morning"; "Good Morning"	11, 12
b'tei-avon	enjoy your meal	"B'tei-avon"	56
b'vakashah	please	"S'lichah, Todah, B'vakashah"	42
chalom	dreams	"Z'man Lishon"	83
chalulim	vessels	"Thanks, God!"	15
chaverim	friends	"Boker Tov Means Good Morning"; "Shalom Chaverim"	11, 86
(ba)choref	(in the) winter	"Four Seasons"	33
kachol	blue	"Colors in My World"	63
(ba)kayitz	(in the) summer	"Four Seasons"	33
l'hitraot	see you later	"Shalom Chaverim"	86
mensch	good person	"Be a Mensch"	80
mezuzah	doorpost	"I See a Mezuzah"	36
HaMotzi blessing		"B'tei-avon"	56
modeh ani	I give thanks	"God Made All Living Things"	8
n'kavim	openings	"Thanks, God!"	15
ozen	ear	"My Body Is Part of Me"	22
peh	mouth	"My Body Is Part of Me"	22
regel	leg	"My Body Is Part of Me"	22
rosh	head	"My Body Is Part of Me"	22
shalom	hello, goodbye, peace	"Boker Tov Means Good Morning"; "Shalom Shalom"; "Z'man Lishon"; "Shalom Chaverim"	11, 18, 83, 86
sh'ma	listen	"Wake Up Sh'ma"	5
s'lichah	I'm sorry, excuse me	"S'lichah, Todah, B'vakashah"	42
(ba)s'tav	(in the) fall	"Four Seasons"	33

Word	Meaning	Song	Page
Tishrei	a Jewish month	"Dance of the Months"	29
todah	thank you	"S'lichah, Todah, B'vakashah"	42
Torah	Five Books of Moses	"The Torah"	39
tzahov	yellow	"Colors in My World"	63
tzedakah	charity	"Tzedakah"	69
yad	hand	"My Body Is Part of Me"	22
yarok	green	"Colors in My World"	53
Yom Chamishi	Thursday	"Days of the Week"	25
Yom Rishon	Sunday	"Days of the Week"	25
Yom R'vi-i	Wednesday	"Days of the Week"	25
Yom Shabbat	Saturday	"Days of the Week"	25
Yom Sheini	Monday	"Days of the Week"	25
Yom Shishi	Friday	"Days of the Week"	25
Yom Sh'lishi	Tuesday	"Days of the Week"	25
zeh z'man lishon	it's time to sleep	"Z'man Lishon"	83